Bass-Ackward Business:

The Power of Helping Without Hustling

by Steve Beecham

Bass-Ackward Business

Published By
Home Town Marketing

ISBN-13: 978-1-43926-943-5

www.unibook.com

INTRODUCTION

Are you tired of going to networking meetings, cold calling, buying leads, or knocking on doors? Would you like for all of your customers to believe you're the greatest thing since sliced bread and never question your cost or abilities? What if you had a proven method for making business come to you? If you're looking for a revolutionary way of doing business, then this book is for you.

Steve Beecham has created a never-ending referral machine. People want to do business with him because he sincerely cares about them. He helps customers with their personal needs -- promoting their areas of expertise to others within his village -- and they love him for it. When you follow Steve's simple yet revolutionary approach to building your business, life becomes more enjoyable and wealth building opportunities present themselves freely. Your world comes alive and it becomes fun to meet new people. Steve has learned that it can be highly profitable to simply spend all your time caring for other people in your "village."

Contents

Preface

What Is The Bass-Ackward Way?

I'm a mortgage broker and in my industry looking out for Number One is the norm—it makes you more money. But to me, this approach lacks authenticity. Making cold calls all day does little more than build a stacked Rolodex full of "No, thank you" and "I'm not interested." So I began searching for a new way to do business.

But my search did not provide the epiphany that forever changed my work approach; it was a serendipitous encounter with a well-known redneck that sent me reeling. It was a solution that put an end to my cold calling and began to create an environment where people called me.

I was excited about this new business revelation. I even developed a unique system that helped me keep track of all the people I was connecting with. But after talking with a couple of friends we discovered that it was more than just a clever way to keep track of clients' information and it was more than just being intentional about keeping in constant contact with people. It was the way I did business.

While most people focus on the bottom line as their main business driver, I focus on building relationships. While most people burn hours away cold calling, I spend time helping people find roofers or painters or a guy to hang a ceiling fan. While most people attend community functions to hand out as many business cards as they can, I attend them in order to strike up deep conversations with one person—trying to find out their passions (expertise) and personal needs (their pains).

After discussing this with my friends one guy said, "Man —Beech, your whole business model is bass-ackward! It really doesn't make sense in the typical business world and yet it's highly successful. I think you're on to something."

We then began outlining this bass-ackward way to do business. What did it mean? How was it different? How could people adapt it for their own businesses? … their own lives? This book is my attempt to package my bass-ackward way to do business.

My hope is that by reading the book you will make helping others a profitable sales technique—and you will want to be bass-ackward like me. Not to be a Beecham clone—God knows one of me is enough—but to be a person others come to because they know you genuinely desire to help them.

The bass-ackward way is a fresh way to approach life, do business and have fun all at the same time. It's the only way I know how to live … bass-ackward.

Chapter 1

Bass-Ackward Business:

The Power of Helping without Hustling

This is a story about a nobody finding gold.

I have never considered myself a brilliant businessman, but I also never thought I'd be a business failure. After college, I figured I was wise enough to recognize a good opportunity when I saw one … so I started a business with my mom.

I'm a simple guy and so I called our traditional clothing store "Beecham's" and left it at that. Something less identifying might have been better. To keep the story short, we worked our butts off and made no money—for eight years. That's about the time I realized my two years experience in mall retail probably wasn't enough. I called a friend to help us conduct a going-out-of-business sale.

After that I started a recycling business. This was before Earth Day and before recycling was cool. I brought on a wealthy partner to keep it afloat and quickly learned that the one with the money makes the rules. He had the money and I lost the business to him.

3

About that time, things became interesting. Like everyone, I wanted a job I could enjoy. But I also wanted to control my own destiny. I'm not cut out to be a "yes" man so I went on a search while my savings dwindled.

I married my college sweetheart and we decided to buy a house. A friend sent me to his brother who was a mortgage broker. The man tried to hire me for the mortgage business but I insisted I didn't want to be a banker and, after the failed retail venture, I was done wearing a tie. Then at a party that evening a good friend named Hal confessed he'd just been fired. He said for his next job he wanted to work for a company where the guys liked to hunt. I told him there were fish and deer heads on the mortgage broker's wall and Hal called him and was hired the next week.

A few weeks later, Hal called to thank me for "the greatest job" he'd ever had. He was making a killing. Like a good opportunist, I investigated.

The country was experiencing one of the greatest refinance booms of all time. Then, for the love of money, I jumped in with both feet. Unfortunately, the refinance well dried up before my feet got wet. I went six months without a deal and when I finally did close one, it was for my brother's home.

It didn't make much sense to remain where I was but at that point I was tired of changing careers and I genuinely liked the mortgage industry, despite my bent towards destitution. So instead of starting over, I set out to find a way to make the business work. This is when my fate started to turn.

A Glimmer of Hope

I'd tried all the popular sales tactics so I knew I needed an approach to business that transcended the norms. One that could weather the unpredictable economy. One that would allow me to feel good about myself and really help people … and make me money more often than every six months.

I started asking questions of all the successful businesspeople who would give me an interview. What were their secrets? What did they do that set them apart? Of the various strategies out there, I discovered three that every one of them applied well:

1. Regular exposure: They all routinely put themselves in places or situations that increased their exposure to potential customers.
2. A well-kept database: They all kept a tight, up-to-date record of everyone they'd done business with.
3. Constant contact: They all had an effective and unpretentious system for staying in touch with their customers.

I was initially interested in only the first strategy because the other two were useless to me until I had customers. So I set out to think about how I could regularly get in front of potential customers; in particular, to people who needed home loans. Were there clubs I should join? Local networking luncheons I could attend? Online sites of which I should become a member? Just about that time, a nugget of inspiration came my way.

The Golden Touch

One morning I got a call at work from my wife Mary. She told me that one of my all-time favorite comedians, Jeff Foxworthy, was speaking at our kids' school and that I might want to hurry down to hear him. I checked my schedule and … I didn't check my schedule. I was in the company Hummer in a split-second making a beeline for the school.

Wouldn't you know it, I was late! But guess who was walking out to the parking lot as I was headed in? You got it. As soon as Jeff saw me he cracked on me. "Man, you just missed one of the best-ever assembly speeches."

In case you missed it, this was Jeff Foxworthy who doesn't know me from Adam, making me feel right at home by ribbing me a bit.

I tried to think of a clever way to introduce myself but it just came out, "Hi, Jeff. Nice to meet you." What happened next surprised me. Before I could get another word in, Jeff started asking me questions:

> *"Do you have kids in the school? Do they like the school?"*
>
> *"What are your kids' names?"*
>
> *"You sound like you're from around here. Where'd you grow up?"*
>
> *"What do you do for a living?"*
>
> *"What high school did you go to?"*

I started to get the feeling that he actually cared about what I was saying. This pattern—him asking, me answering—continued a few more minutes until we both had to go. I left the encounter feeling ten feet tall. I thought Jeff Foxworthy was the coolest celebrity I'd ever met.

Then it hit me. I didn't doubt there were many opportunities to put myself in places where I could land prospects. But I wondered, would any of them make me more memorable than repeating what Jeff did for me?

I could spray business cards across the city like a sprinkler and I could schmooze with the best of them but, frankly, neither got me excited or had a high rate of success. It came down to a matter of taste. Did I want to be known as a schmoozer, a hustler? Or did I want to be known as a great guy and a friend? The decision wasn't difficult.

I wanted to do for others what Jeff Foxworthy did for me. He got to know me with no strings attached and as a result, I liked him. More importantly, I remembered him and wanted to promote him to other people, tell them what a great guy he was. In a subtle and unassuming way, he elevated himself in my mind. I knew that if I could do the same in others' minds by being intentional about getting to know them, by treating them as people and not prospects, they would be much more apt to remember and promote me.

The more I thought about it, the more it excited me. From that fateful day forward, I committed to asking thoughtful questions of every new person I met and every acquaintance I didn't know very well. I'm talking about every person, not just those I considered business prospects—my dentist, my server at the restaurant, my mechanic. My goal was to make them feel good without any strings. I wasn't going to bring up my mortgage business or pester them for a referral at the end of the conversation. I was committed to simply putting them first in conversation. In the back of my mind, I suspected this might at least land me one or two loans indirectly, but I never expected what actually happened.

As I continued on my crusade of propositionless conversations, I began to see a pattern in people's responses. I noticed that everyone either talked about a problem they were trying to solve or an area of expertise they were trying to promote. I decided that instead of just getting to know them and leaving off there, I should begin doing something with their answers. Specifically, I decided to become a problem solver and a promoter. This is when my business began to not only turn around; it began to take off. That was seven years ago and it hasn't let up since.

Striking Gold

There is something magical about reciprocity when it happens naturally. Unfortunately, most of what we're taught about networking, marketing and prospecting removes the magic. It is Cracker Jack trickery masked by professionalism and a five-star smile. The truth is, we approach relationships with prospecting on the brain because we want—we need—the referrals. We join clubs and attend luncheons not to build meaningful friendships but to secure leads and grow our businesses. We give favors only to receive favors in return—cheaper services, quicker turnaround, lucrative connections and so on. The marketplace definition of helping is the word "if." I will scratch your back … if you scratch mine. That's not reciprocity. It's merely bartering—dealing ahead of time—so that both parties get what they want. Natural reciprocity is somewhat unexpected, like a pleasant surprise, even though by human nature we might hope for it. This is the realm from which my business started to bloom.

As I began to find ways to solve the problems people shared with me, those same people began looking for ways to help me. Mark Buelow, a local house remodeler, is an early example.

I met Mark at the Rotary Club. I have a little strategy for the Rotary Club. Each week I try to target one person to really connect with—you know, have a meaningful conversation with. So I was talking to Mark about his business and he communicated to me that he wanted to buy out a certain contractor in order to take his business to the next level. We talked for a while and I gave him some advice on his business ideas and tried to help him add value to what he was trying to do. Our conversation went deep and we both learned a lot about one another.

Fast-forward six months. I need to get some remodeling done. Guess who I call? I give Mark the job and he knocks it out of the park, so naturally I referred him some customers. Since this whole exchange Mark has referred people to me and I've redone his loan twice.

I didn't go into the conversation looking to get something from Mark. Rather, I sought to uncover Mark's expertise—I dug deep to find out what his passions and hobbies were—who he really was. And I left it at that. Things didn't click until months later when I had a need. Because Mark and I had become friends, he came to mind first. I connected his expertise with my need and the rest is history.

I noticed a similar result when I became a promoter of the people I talked to. As conversations turned toward a person's area of expertise, I committed to find an outlet for their skills. At times, this meant making simple connections like referring John, a local carpenter I met and trusted, to my neighbor who needed a reliable, fair-priced deck built on the back of their home. It also meant helping Joe, a local builder, make a successful run for mayor. In both instances, I helped the individuals without mention of business. Yet in both instances, business came to me as a result and in much greater volume than had I offered help on the condition that they return the favor.

Why It Works

My "helping without hustling" strategy is bass-ackward when you compare it to everything I've been taught about building a business. It also seems risky and unmanageable because it is overly dependent on other people. But the way I saw it in the beginning is how I still see it today: No matter what business you're in, your level of success inescapably, undeniably depends on the actions of other people. And there are only two categories in which we can place people's actions: they are either reactive or proactive.

If the people on whom you are building your business are merely reactive—buying only when you persuade, manipulate or pacify them … and referring others to you only when you remind, urge or beg them—you will always be a slave to clever marketing, advertising and prospecting to keep your business afloat.

On the other hand, if the people on whom you are building your business are proactive—buying out of a genuine indebtedness to you … and referring others to you in unsolicited gratitude, confidence and loyalty—you will no longer need clever, edgy salesmanship to sustain your business. I can say this with confidence. One hundred percent of my business is either repeat or referred customers. Cold calling, prospecting and marketing have been things of the past for many years.

After those first weeks of initiating a helping without hustling approach to relationships, my mortgage business never suffered again. The more people I helped, the more business came in. I'll say it again: There is something magical about helping without strings. Maybe it has something to do with the counter-intuitive nature of the act.

The Power of the Unexpected

Nowadays, people expect that there's an ulterior motive behind every good word or deed. Our lives are bombarded with slogans, gimmicks and salespeople that pose as "help" but actually aim to recruit us for their own purposes. I know this is why I was so taken aback by Jeff Foxworthy's approach with me. I don't expect celebrities to take a genuine interest in me. I expect them to pay me lip service but genuinely not give a crap. Foxworthy won me over because he was not what I expected.

Helping without hustling works the same way. Everyone out there who has the potential to give you business expects you to ask for it, in one covert way or another:

- "We've got the best customer service"
- A clever advertisement
- A commitment to serve, unique from the thousands of other commitments to serve
- A free lunch with a sales pitch for dessert
- "Can we get together at Starbucks for a cup of coffee?"
- An ever-so-thoughtful gift card (bought in bulk)
- "I'd like you to come to a meeting I'm having …"

… and so on. And unless you're in the business of stealing money from the elderly, your prospects know you're just asking for business in an alluring way. I'll let you in on a secret: If they buy from you, it's rarely because you hooked them with your marketing genius.

Today's consumers are educated enough that they aren't so ignorantly sold. They have all the information they need at their Internet-ready fingertips and when they go to buy, many already know what they want. The best you can do with a good come-on is not turn them completely off.

I didn't want to compete on the playing field of gimmicks, slogans and two-sided promises. I wanted to feel good about myself every morning and, come evening, know I did somebody good. I never imagined helping without hustling would become a legitimate business strategy, but when I consider what the competition is doing, its success makes sense.

People are so surprised by a person who doesn't have an ulterior motive that they never forget you, they tell others about you and they want to help you in return. For some, what I'm saying is probably too vague. "What are the ROI numbers?" they ask. Well, the answer is only this: I now have approximately 10,000 people in my personal network—and I did eventually implement the other two strategies I gleaned; a well-kept database and constant contact, which we'll talk about in coming chapters —but outside of my large network, I can't give you definitive numbers except to say that I don't have to worry about business coming in. How's that for stress management?

Every day my office receives approximately 30 calls. One-quarter of them are people asking for help that has nothing to do with a mortgage. "Where can I get my car fixed?" "What restaurant should I take my in-laws to?" "Who should I call for life insurance?" These people call me because in the metro Atlanta area, I've become known as the go-to guy, the most connected guy in town. I didn't get that way by holding "free" mortgage seminars or erecting a large billboard featuring my confident, trustworthy face. I got that way by helping people without hustling them for business. I help everyone I can, too—not just those I perceive as potential gold mines. Now, they and their families and friends trust me to solve their problems, promote their expertise … and do their mortgages.

The other three-quarters of my daily calls are from people I helped or friends of people I helped looking for a home loan. Sometimes I have to think back months to recall the string-free help that made them remember me. Other times I helped them just the other day. But the point is not how often or how quickly they offer me their business. If I had time to waste, I could probably come up with the percentage of people I helped who turn into customers and the average timeframe in which this happens, but those things don't matter to me. They shouldn't matter to you.

What matters is that I'm doing something I love—unconditionally helping people—every day; and it's made me a rich man in business and life. If you want to be sentimental about it, I'm creating a legacy of love, and love, as the popular lyric goes, makes the world go round.

Critics will call me what they will—a character, a naive redneck, a lucky nobody—but those same critics can't deny the power of natural reciprocity in their own lives. No one can. It is why Thoreau wrote, "Goodness is the only investment that never fails." This is as true in business as it is in life.

I'll lay it out for you. If sustainable success and satisfaction are your ultimate goals, shallow motivation won't work and recycled mission statements won't stick. We live in an age of information with consumers far more savvy than we'd like to admit. People are tired of the old business model that portrays the customer as the sheep and the business as the shepherd. Consumers guide themselves now. They see gimmicks a mile away. They run from underhanded approaches. Instead, they gravitate to what is real and lasting. They return to what is honest and worthy. To offer them what they want, we businesspeople need an authentic business foundation—one that restores our faith in what we do each day, and one that restores their faith in human goodness and good business...

I am the first to admit I'm no business genius. I'm just a southerner you've never heard of who figured I'd at least do something worthwhile each day while my third consecutive business dried up. Then I discovered gold. And now, like a good southern host, I want to share the wealth and teach you how to use it. I'm confident it will boom your business and better your life.

A Bass-ackward Revelation

It is possible to help people without hustling them. Or put another way, you can serve others without selling and chances are the amount of reciprocity you experience because of your approach will astound you.

Throughout the rest of this book you will discover how this approach has changed my business and continues to give me dramatic life rewards. It all starts with getting rid of the sales talk and just being yourself. After you're relaxed, you need to realize that it's actually not about you or your sales; it's about helping others. By meeting the needs of others you will invariably experience the rich blessing of reciprocity.

Bass-ackward Nuts-n-Bolts

As we move through the book, take a few moments to check out this section. For those who need these ideas in quick bulleted points, look no further. As we progress through the bass-ackward concept, this section will become more specific as well. Use it as your mini-guide to helping without hustling.

In the first chapter I have set the stage for you to revolutionize the way you do business and live life with a bass-ackward approach. Here are your nuts-n-bolts:

- Become the go-to guy or gal in your local sphere of influence—the mayor of your village.
- As you become the mayor and begin attending commu-

---

nity gatherings, zero in on one person to really go deep with.

- Start deep, authentic conversations with people.
  - ◦ Connect with people on a personal level by asking them about their lives—what gets them excited, what concerns them.
  - ◦ People will love you when you show genuine concern and care for them.
  - ◦ Get your conversations to hit the "friendship trigger" —that place where they trust you enough to be your friend.
  - ◦ A friend will want to do business with you. The value of trust is immeasurable.
- In these conversations seek to find out the areas of pain in the person's life or what their area of expertise is.
- Find a way to meet their need OR to connect them with someone who can.
- Remember, the name of the game is to help, help, help. No strings attached.

Many reading this are shuddering at the thought of going deep with someone. Just think to yourself: "What would I love someone to ask me?" or "What do I love talking about?" We are all eerily similar in this regard. We all have similar things that really get us going or things that we are worried about. Find those things in the person you are talking with. It usually only takes one good question and the rest takes care of itself.

Chapter 2

The Goal: Become the Mayor of Your Village

"Everyone thinks of changing the world, but no one thinks of changing himself."
—Leo Tolstoy

Pubs get a bad rap. In the U.S. we call them bars and we all know what our parents thought about bars. But the original bars were the public houses of ancient Rome. The Roman public houses were multifaceted places providing spirits, lodging, even entertainment. Over time public houses became known as "pubs." In England pubs were used as the "third place," the place between home and work where everyone would connect.

Here in America, Starbucks has become the proverbial third place—the place we go to have coffee, meet with friends, hear some new music, or conduct business. It's that place in between home and work.

17

But the big difference in our culture is that we have to drive some-where to find that third place. In the good old days, people stopped by the village pub on their way home from work. Pubs were the heartbeat of the community; everyone stopped in for a drink, some good con-versation or to hear the latest news. It's not hard to see how commu-nities that were tied together by a common gathering place enjoyed a sense of intimacy that we have lost in our hurry-up culture.

Like any small American town, these old villages had mayors. Oftentimes the mayor in these communities would be the "go-to guy"—the guy or gal you'd run into at the pub who could answer all your questions, help you find work or stop by to check on the farm when you were out of town. Even in modern times, an English mayor's role is focused less on governing and more on civic duties and the advancement of the public welfare.

To know the mayor in these old villages was to be on the inside. Not only did you know someone you could trust to look out for the good of the community but this person also knew you. Boy, what hap-pened to the good old days?

This kind of connectedness is the heart of the bass-ackward busi-ness approach. It's the idea that you need to be intentional about being involved in people's lives. You have to be where people are in your community—those third places—to find out what's going on in their lives. You can't stay secluded in your business life or personal life. You need to go out of your way to be the "mayor of your commu-nity."

I love it when someone says, "I'll call Beech, because he knows everybody." If people are saying things like that, then word is get-ting around that I am helping people—meeting their needs. When you help others, it is positive for you. That friend who sought you out because you are the go-to guy or gal knows that you know folks. And they, in turn, will tell their friends about how they were helped by you. The more your name comes up, the more business you do.

I know this may sound like just another way to market yourself or create networks, but it's more than that. When you are real with people—when you are the mayor of your community, or sphere of influence —word gets around. It's natural and it's based on the fact that you are building massive trust equity in your community. This is invaluable—not just for business, but for all of life.

Before you start hem-hawin' around and complaining about how much time it's going to take to get involved in your community, let me explain something. Being the mayor of your village does mean being active in your community—being involved in places where the people are. But the first thing you should do before you go out and join the local Rotary Club is concentrate on your own sphere of influence.

Start small. Who are the people you know now? Who are the people you run into all the time? These people are your sphere of influence. Maybe you're like me and you eat at the same diner three times a week, or perhaps you have a group that gets together once a week at another fine dining establishment. That's your sphere of influence—your village.

The people you encounter daily are the ones you should concentrate on helping first. As you begin to help them, word will get around to their friends.

"Oh, you need a good roofer? You should call my buddy Beech. That crazy guy knows everyone—he helped us find a great roofer and painter for our investment property."

That's the kind of conversation you want to be a part of without being there! As your reputation grows in your immediate community, it will begin to influence those outside of your community. Do you see now how this idea works? Good. Keep reading—it gets better!

Now before you get all jazzed up thinking, "Hey, I can do this. Helping people is easy—and what a great strategy!" take a step back. As we move through my little "system," remember this is about helping without hustling. You may be tempted to incorporate some of these "best practices" without understanding the heart behind it.

I'm communicating this approach to you in this way—these steps—because it's the easiest way to get the idea across. You, however, cannot simply program this new approach into your sales repertoire.

Remember, being the mayor of your village is about meeting people's needs where they are. That's it. No strings attached. So please check your ego at the door and consider how you can be that go-to guy or gal that people think of when they are in a bind and really need something.

Organic Madness

Now is the best time to be organic—especially if you happen to be a cucumber or tomato. But we aren't talking vegetables here; we're talking people. And even though our culture has a healthy love affair with "organic this" and "organic that" we would do well to seek out some organic community.

For something to be organic it has to be grown in a pure environment—no pesticides or enhancers. It's the same with cultivating relationships. When everything else in life falls away, relationships are all that are left, but so often we treat them like they are "opportunities" or a "next step" to our business gold mine. We need to be real with each other. We need to care about each other. And we need to do this because it's the right thing to do, not because it will fatten our bottom line.

My conversation with Jeff Foxworthy flipped a switch in my mind. If a celebrity can talk with me—Steve Beecham—and make me feel like I matter, what's my excuse? Right off the bat, Jeff made our conversation deeper by making me a priority. I didn't feel manipulated. I felt important. When people interact in this way a special bond is created; that bond is built on trust. People call me up to ask about a good garage to take their car to because they trust me; they know that chances are I know a good garage guy. They trust that I'll steer them in the right direction.

Just the other day a friend I met at the Rotary Club emailed me and asked if I could help him locate a reputable roofer. I get hundreds of emails a day and many of them are just like this one: someone in need. My sphere of influence—my village—continues to expand and it's not because I am pounding the streets or making cold calls. It's because people know I care.

Remember, relationships are not products to be mass-produced for the sake of a sale. They are special portals into the lives of others. If you approach relationships without pretense (pesticides) or a manipulative "angle" (enhancers) then you are on your way to cultivating a fresh organic community—and you are the mayor of that community.

Expand Your Horizons

But it's not just about your community. When you make the effort needed to stick your neck out there to become a bass-ackward mayor, your community is just the beginning. Sooner or later your influence will extend into your city, possibly the country—even into your global village.

I meet new people every day right here in metro Atlanta. I'm out cultivating organic community, trying to find ways to help those I come in contact with. Eventually those relationships blossom beyond the community.

Take Lee, for example. Lee now lives in Knoxville but he is still part of my "expanded" community. Because I took the time to build a relationship with Lee and to give him some helpful tips, he is now reciprocating the helping without hustling mindset from Tennessee (I'm still not a Vols fan, though!). Here's a letter I received from Lee that says it all.

> *Dear Steve,*
>
> *I want to thank you for being a mentor and sharing a bit of wisdom that would have probably taken me years to acquire. If you recall, I recently called you to tell you how proud of myself I was for finally walking into a realtor's office that had intimidated me, and you asked me if I had gotten any referrals and how I had offered to help them.*
>
> *You told me the key to being successful has three components: get out of the office, focus on relationships, and find a way to help people. You told me the most important thing I can do is to figure out how to help people.*
>
> *When I moved to Knoxville from Atlanta, I was worried that I would not be able to get referrals from*

real estate agents because the market is different, and for two months I was right. I got out of the office and focused on creating relationships, but I felt as though something was missing. I was persistent and I was really proud when I got past the gatekeeper of one of the best agents in town, so I called you on a Wednesday to tell you of my success. That is when you asked me how I was able to help them. You suggested that I offer to help market their properties by giving them exposure in my newsletter. I resolved to do just that.

On Thursday, I called the office manager to tell her that I had something that I needed to bring by and to ask what time the office closed. She told me that the office closed at five but that she and the owner/broker was usually there a bit later. I stopped by at 4:45p, dropped off a basket of candy for the receptionist and when I brought the office manager's basket to her, she told me to hang out for a minute because she thought the broker would be off the phone and that I should introduce myself.

When he got off the phone, he walked into the office where I was standing and I introduced myself. I told him that I liked his website and wondered if it would be okay if I featured his development in my newsletter that goes out to my entire database of about 2,500 people. He said sure, but that he had a new development that I might be more interested in as he motioned me into his office.

23

We sat down and talked for about 20 minutes about his new development, and I left with a disk full of items I could use to help him get exposure for it.

The next day, Friday, at 4:30 pm I got a phone call from a customer who was working with this agent that had intimidated me for two months. On Monday, I got two more phone calls. And, all it took was a genuine offer of assistance. When I close these loans, I will be sure to send you a box of chocolates.

One more thing, if you need anything, let me know, and if you don't mind, I would like to feature your lake house rental in my next newsletter.
Let me know how I can help.

Sincerely,
Lee

As your relationship base grows, so does your sphere of influence. My mortgage company is based in a nice Atlanta suburb, but my influence reaches beyond the mortgage industry. I've influenced the political arena by throwing a fundraising party for a candidate. Just by taking the time to write this book I'm influencing your industry with my bass-ackward mindset.

We all have grandiose dreams of growing our networks to massive proportions. It's natural to desire success in your industry. But too often it is the pursuit of "the big" that causes us to look past "the small."

That Won't Work For Me

Many of my friends work for national corporations and can't understand how being the mayor of their village will help them on a national account. But to them I say that this concept is extremely helpful.

Say your neighbor—we'll call him Rob—knows Sam, who is the CEO of one of the companies you want to get connected with. If you help Rob in the simplest way, it could open up lines of communication that could put you in contact with Sam. I've found that if you just start talking to people—finding out what they do and what they need—you'll be surprised at how connected we all really are.

But there are always doubters. My friend Mark, for example, works for a Fortune 500 software company. He always asks me, "Beech, how is being the mayor of my village going to help me make a sale in New York or L.A. or Seattle?" So I tell him, "Well, Mark, your neighborhood is filled with guys who are top-level executives. But you'll never know what companies they work for if you don't get into a deep conversation with one of them."

The reality is that there is probably someone in Mark's neighborhood who works for or knows someone who works for one of the companies that he wants to connect with. A simple conversation could make all the difference.

My friend Trip says he just needs to focus on local insurance companies. But I convinced him that if he just got to know people in his sphere of influence—people outside of the insurance company world—it would reap more benefits for him than cold calling all day long.

Trip doesn't think that getting to know people in his sphere of influence will help him get business. But what Trip doesn't understand is that if he would just poke around, he would run into someone who he could refer someone else to or even find business himself.

I don't mean to belabor the point, but everybody you know can help you. You think that because you do work outside of your community that getting to know people inside your community won't get you more business. But the reality is this: Getting to know people in your community can be the connector to those very people you want to meet.

Think Big, But Start Small

Keep your goals for broad exposure ever on your mind, but focus your efforts on the opportunities right in front of you. Remember, your first goal is to be the mayor of your village. The best way to meet new people is to involve yourself in your community. The important thing to remember is that you should only get involved with something that you are genuinely interested in. Or you may want to get involved with something that involves your children, like coaching a team or leading a Boy or Girl Scout Troop. That way, your community involvement time is also family time.

Boy, talk about organic community. If you start pouring yourself into your children and their activities within the community, the rewards will be evidenced in their lives. It's like the "pay it forward" idea. Your children see you caring for them and their goals and dreams. Your spouse notices how much you care for them and for families connected to the team. All of a sudden your actions are rubbing off on your whole family and they begin to go deep with their friends. The domino effect is in full force now. Congratulations! You are now a highly influential mayor of the number one community on your list—your family.

Modeling not only builds trust with your family but it galvanizes the perspectives of others in your community. People see you out with your kids playing and getting involved—it inspires them to do it and it makes you approachable. You've just earned their trust.

Cliques Are So Fourth Grade

As you involve yourself in community-oriented groups, keep in mind that just joining won't do you much good. You should go in with a strategy to create visibility and face time with as many members as possible. If you join a civic group, volunteer to serve on and lead committees. Give people the opportunity to get to know you. If you belong to a club with a hundred or more members, it is easier to get visibility if you're leading the meeting than if you're always seated at the back of the room with the same group of friends each week.

This brings up another important point: cliques. Don't fall into the trap of sitting with the same group of people each week. Move around and meet new people each week. Try to target one member a week that you have lunch with, and if possible linger after the meeting and dig deep with them. Try to find out how you can help them.

You must fight the urge to stay in that nice comfort zone with the people that are most familiar to you. For people to know who you are and what you do, they need to know you care.

Remember how you felt in grade school when all the "cool" people sat together at lunch? Not a good feeling. But more importantly, sticking to your good buddy network doesn't get you anywhere. You're just scratching the same backs all the time. When we seek out ways to help those we come in contact with, we exponentially increase our personal network, our influence and--here's the kicker--we grow as individuals enriched by the lives of others.

Bass-Ackward Nuts-n-Bolts

A good mayor knows how to connect with people. Here are some practical things to keep in mind as you meet new people and expand your sphere of influence:

- Business can come to you from 360 degrees. Everyone you know has the potential to send you business.
- Make a list of everyone you know. What this means is that if someone calls you and needs a plumber you need to be able to bring up the number of a good plumber.
- Don't skimp on your list. List out everyone: your mother, your mechanic, your dentist, your neighbor, former associates … everyone!
- When you meet someone add them to your list.
  - With today's technology it is simple to find a program (like Outlook) that will sync with your phone. This makes storing and organizing your contacts simple and fast. The more computer literate you are, the more sophisticated the program can be, but I try and keep it simple. Most computer programs will allow you to search your database multiple ways—by name or address—but I always try to put in all the pertinent information up front. This makes my searching easy.

- You just can't add a name and forget about it. You have to keep this information as up to date as possible, so make changes to it as your customers move or change jobs. If it helps, organize them by vocation or simply file them alphabetically; whatever works for you.

- Establish the way you want to stay in contact with your list so you will know what info to put in your database. This is critical. Don't collect info you're not going to use; it will become too time consuming. If you find you need the information later, it gives you an excuse to reconnect with the contact.

- When you call someone to re-discuss their pain or pleasure you will become someone he or she will remember—because you cared. Always reconnect to discuss the other person's pains and pleasure.

Bass-Ackward Community Mayor

As the mayor of your village you are the go-to guy or gal. This is true because people know that you actually care about them. And that you do it with no strings attached. They see you at community events, they see you involved with your family and they watch you coach their kids at soccer. People in the community trust you. As a result, your phone rings off the hook because you make it your business to pour yourself into the lives of others. You are a community mayor—it's bass-ackward and it feels great!

29

***

In the next few chapters we will dig a bit deeper into my bass-ackward strategy of helping without hustling. Remember as you move through this that your goal is to become the mayor of your village—your sphere of influence. Ultimately, you will expand that influence locally and beyond. Some of you may be a bit apprehensive to get involved in the community and be the go-to guy or gal, but I've broken down the process to make it simple and fun.

Let's take another look at the conversation that started it all for me. The nuggets I gleaned from that conversation radically changed my outlook for developing relationships and running my business. Maybe it will help change your perspective too .

Chapter 3

Step One: Propositionless Conversations

"Let us make a special effort to stop communicating with each other, so we can have some conversation."
—Mark Twain

Talk to Me!

I can't get over how curt our culture is. People just don't care about other people anymore. Have you ever entered into a conversation with someone, only to quickly discover they were just putting on a front? After you leave the conversation you realize they didn't care to talk to you and could not have cared less about what you had to say. I hate that feeling.

In the business world there is an almost hidden language that communicates fluff--and everyone is fine with it. We've all attended the lunch meeting just to "connect." The table conversation is light. There is fake laughter and feigned interest by all parties. Drifting eyes

31

tell you that the other person can't wait to end the conversation and get on with the sale.

So you order an espresso and some pie and brace yourself for the "sell." This is what I call a propositioned conversation. It's the language of the day, and for some strange reason we are all fine with it.

We set up our meetings, finely tuned to plug someone with a nice-sized proposition. "Hey Marty, thanks for hooking up for lunch. I really enjoyed the conversation. Could I run something by you?" This conversation tag cheapens everything. It basically tells the other person the only reason they are sitting at the table is because you want to get something from them. Raise your hand if you like that feeling. That's what I thought. It's time to change things up a bit.

Do You Care?

On the other hand some people don't even waste time with the hidden business language. They think they can "woo" you with their sales savvy or whatever you want to call it. Everything is transactional up front. At least this way you know you're not being schmoozed, but it's just as sleazy.

Let me give you an example. I was teaching the "helping without hustling" principles to my staff in a meeting, when out of the blue an insurance salesman just walks in—no call, no introduction; he just interrupts. And when I say "interrupts," what I mean is this guy opens up the door to my office, comes in and starts trying sell me. In front of my own staff! After I picked my jaw up from the floor, I engaged.

He handed me his card and then proceeded to tell me about how great he was; he could get my customers the best prices and he was the "mortgage king." You get the picture. As he continued to praise himself up and down, I started laughing. This was exactly what I was telling my staff not to do!

So I asked him, "What's in it for me?"

"I will put you on my milk route—come by on a regular basis," he replied.

"But what's in it for me, the mortgage guy?" I pressed.

"I'll give your customers great services and rates."

"But where is my benefit?" I interrupted. "What's in it for Steve Beecham?"

He just didn't get it. Of course I want my customers to get a good deal, but why would I use him over another agent? I took this opportunity to explain that it was important to care about me, the loan officer—I should be his customer.

If he wanted me to send him business I needed to know that he valued me. I needed to know how his service would benefit me. Did he even care? Or was I just part of his bottom line?

But he wasn't interested in me, just in getting to my customers— he just wanted my business. To him, I was a step towards something else. Why would I want to enter into a business relationship with a guy who did not value me, aside from how I could help him?

As he left I looked at my team and told them to consider how they come across to their real estate agents: "You call them and tell them you have great rates and service, but so does everyone. How are you different? What's in it for the agent? That agent is the one who is going to send you the customer; therefore they are your customer."

You will never know what's in it for someone unless you ask them enough questions. It all starts from a real conversation that shows you care more for them than your bottom line—no propositions. Find out how you can help someone and you, inevitably, will find that trust and strong relationships are not far behind.

But be careful. You can start what you think is a meaningful conversation and end up blabbing the whole time. And most people will let you do it! Just because there was a conversation doesn't mean there was a connection. Be self-aware and zip it if you feel like you're carrying the conversation. This is when it is invaluable to ask good questions. If you are armed with good questions and dig deep into the other person, then chances are you will make a good connection.

The average person may look like or even act like they don't want to talk, but the truth is most people love to talk about their family or job or what they did last weekend. We are a therapy-happy society; we love talking about our problems and figuring out how to solve them. Now, I'm not suggesting you get a counseling degree or anything like that. All I'm saying is that most people are happy to have a meaningful conversation; they just need a little push.

If It Feels Good, Do It

The sixties and seventies were a time of "freedom." With "free love" at the epicenter of the mainstream mindset, people were governed by the "If it feels good, do it!" mantra. This way of thinking has obvious repercussions to it—and I mean negative ones. But at the heart of this mentality is the truth that all people like to feel good. No one enjoys feeling bad or stupid or alone.

But too often we care little of what others think in the business world. We are driven by our performance metrics and, more importantly, how much money we will gain from the sale or the potential network associated with a single person. We need to move away from this way of thinking.

Perhaps one way to move beyond the typical "business conversation" is to ask yourself a simple question: "How would I want to feel in this situation?" Or, to put it another way: "If it would feel good to me, say it!"

We all grew up with the golden rule. How many times did we hear our parents tell us to "do unto others as we would have them do to us"? Funny how those little axioms from childhood creep up on you! But it's true. Would you want to feel like a business piñata—just used for what people can get out of you? I'm sure it's no fun to be a piñata. Those things get the snot whacked out of them. Likewise, it's no fun to be used. You would want someone to care about you, what you thought and how life was treating you.

This is what made my experience with Jeff Foxworthy so surprising. While I was angling for a nice one-liner to pry open a business conversation, he was busy getting to know me. While I was deciding how to "play" the encounter, he was busy asking about my kids and my family. While I was busy feeling like a jackass, he was grinning his appreciation for our conversation. Man, are you kidding me? Jeff taught me a hard lesson.

I left that conversation feeling special. It's funny how a little authenticity and care can enrich our interactions with one another. This lesson changed my perspective on how I approach my business and, more importantly, how I cultivate relationships.

What do you think would have happened if I had approached Jeff with some silly quip and really pushed my business on him? He would not have felt valued. More than likely he is used to people trying to use him. But how many people really pursue him? How many people treat him like they would one of their friends?

The bottom line is we need to think about our conversations in terms of what would make the other person feel good—or, more importantly, what would make the other person feel valued. When your intent for a conversation is to gain rather than help, people pick up on that. They sense you are not being empathetic and only care about your own needs.

Fragments of Ourselves

Have you ever had an acquaintance or friend who was a chameleon? You know, the kind of person you might run into in the church halls and then again on the basketball court or at the high school football game and each time you run into them they are somebody completely different. It's easy to do. People are always saying, "Well, I'm going to put my business hat on now." Are you like this?

It's understandable to think that we need to "put on" a different persona for work, family and play. I get it. Most people do it to insulate their lives. But then how are we supposed to find out who anyone is if we are all out there pretending to be something we're really not?

We need to de-segment our lives. Helping without hustling is a way of life that is built on seeking the greater good for your fellow man. We have been programmed to turn on our "business" personas for so long that we forget to turn them off. But perhaps they need to stay off.

What if we approached all of life the same way: seeking ways to help others? No fronts, no "hats" … just the honest-to-goodness me and the honest-to-goodness you. I believe we would see not only a business revolution, but personal revolutions happening all over our communities.

I try to be me all the time. This way people know what they're getting. Whether I'm at my cabin, on my dirt bike or selling mortgages, I'm Steve Beecham. I try to cut the posturing and manipulation out of my life and replace it with thoughtful care for those around me. Does it always pay off? No. But that's the point. Helping without hustling is you caring for me and vice versa because it's a better way to live. I know who I am. Who are you?

Moving Past The Propositions

"Ok, Steve, this sounds great—all this buttery talk about helping others and not being self-serving. I get it. But how do I pull it off?"

I thought you'd never ask. Admittedly, it seems simple but leaving propositions out of our business conversations is tough. We have been ingrained with the "me first" mentality. We think that we gain power through leverage and we typically use people like pawns, leveraging them when we should be pouring ourselves into them.

I've got an idea that will help you think through your business conversations. This isn't an exact science because people are so unique, but I think this idea will help lay a foundation for you:

Give Yourself - Enter each conversation with the intent to help the other person. This is a departure from how you/we are used to talking to people but it is a vital first step. When people know you care, you build trust. And trust is the foundation to truly deep relationships. Giving of yourself needs to be your focus here. You need to do all you can to resist the temptation to capitalize on a so-called opportunity. Help first.

The End of Cold Calls

If you're like me then you think cold calling in sales is about as fun as a root canal. It's the epitome of the propositioned conversation. Actually, it's worse than that. People are automatically wary of the conversation, knowing that you're trying to sell them something. What's even worse is the way you feel after you've done a few calls with no leads. Who needs it?

If you're bass-ackward like me, you don't need it. This whole approach to communicating with people in an authentic way sidesteps all that sales junk. When you begin building relationships, people start coming to you—they start introducing you to new people. Before long you have more legitimate leads than you know what to do with. And yet you sought none of it. You sought to help someone; with pure motives you found a way to meet the needs or celebrate the gifts of others.

To me, the interesting thing here is that we aren't really discussing sales and business tactics. Rather, we are discussing a better way to live. And this way influences every other part of life: work, family, friends, church, and community. Everything.

The only reason we ever needed something like cold calling was because we had forgotten how to be friends with people. We have become so self-centered and isolated in our lives that the only way we know how to treat others is as a means to an end.

This isn't living—it's a lonely way to make money. In the end, the money and material possession fade away. The only things that last forever are our relationships with people. Like an old friend once told me: "Use things, love people—not the other way around."

Bass-Ackward Conversations

Let's put an end, once and for all, to lame conversations that are only self-serving. Let's reach beyond the typical "me-first" mentality of business and test a new way to grow business—by growing relationships.

38

Bass-Ackward Nuts-n-Bolts

Here are some tips to help you go deep with people.

- To be a friend you must truly be concerned with people. This cannot be faked. Concentrate on listening rather than talking. Be in the conversation.
- You need to ask the same questions your mom would ask if she were meeting one of your friends for the first time. "Where do you live? What do you do for a living? Tell me about your family." You get the idea.
- When you ask those deep personal questions, don't be afraid to continue down those conversational paths. If the conversation goes into their hobbies or interests, stay on that line of thought. Ask questions about how they got into that hobby or how it makes them feel. Go deep!
- Think of the conversation as similar to being on a blind date. What would you ask the other person in order to get to know them better?
- Look people in the EYE. Yeah, and by "eye," I mean their left eye. Typically when you're talking to someone about serious matters or business affairs, you look into their right eye. Looking into their left eye communicates sincerity—they will feel like you care.

I never have a need for cold calling anymore because I have too many relationships to keep up with. This is a good problem to have! To help people without hustling them you must be tuned in to their needs. You discover people's needs through direct and deep conver-

39

sations that probe. Ultimately, it's about making others feel valued instead of used.

***

The main way I'm able to take conversations deeper is to find out what a person's needs are. In the next chapter we will explore ways to discover the needs of others and what to do once you find them. You can't help someone if you don't know their "hurts." You can't promote someone's expertise if you don't know what it is.

Chapter 4

Step Two: Discover Sally's Pain or Mel's Expertise

"Unless someone like you cares a whole awful lot, nothing is going to get better. It's not." —Dr. Seuss

Helping Just Because

When you think of Mother Teresa, the first thing you think of is her focus on helping others. She gave her life over to working with children who, by the world's standards, had no hope. What drove someone like Mother Teresa to give of herself in such a deep capacity? It is easy to watch a television show and see others who are helping the needy all over the world and be totally untouched by it. Sure, we recognize how great someone like Mother Teresa was, but just knowing about her usually doesn't change us. We turn back to our steak and potatoes, sip our merlot and finish the paper.

But then there are some of us who have firsthand experience helping others; perhaps through a community event—like a fundraiser—or possibly a mission trip with our church, or maybe we spent some time visiting a nursing home during the Christmas holidays. Whatever the experience, once we've done it, we "get it." There is something infectious about helping others. No leverage, no propositions; just a pure desire to see someone's circumstances improve.

When you try to explain it to someone, words fail. Simply put, there is something transcendent about helping others. It's like we were all wired to care for others and when that wire is tapped, endless energy is released—making us want more of the same. All humans have an innate sense of community that drives us toward one another. Sometimes our culture gets in the way of that; sometimes our occupations remove the human element altogether, caring only for the bottom line.

And yet most of us will attest to the fact that when we are too often removed from our fellow man we feel adrift—needing that human touch. When we get our hands dirty in the community and really start helping others, we feel alive again. That transcendent feeling returns and we can rest our heads at night knowing that yes, we are indeed still human.

Ladies And Gentlemen

But as I stated at the end of the previous chapter, this transcendence or power is lost when we allow our lives to be governed by propositions. Specifically to our topic here, when propositions dictate our conversations, then our relationships become frail. People are relegated to a mere potential sale and they know it. They can feel it!

So how can we remove this characteristic from our professional life? How can the salesman continue to sell while keeping his humanity? How can the secretary truly look out for others while maintaining high productivity standards? At some point we all dig in and "git'r done," but so often that leaves people feeling trampled. We need to start treating one another as humans—individuals are much more than a bottom line.

I once checked into a Ritz-Carlton. Now first of all, you have to know that this wasn't my first time at the Ritz, it was a return stay, and boy, were my eyes opened. When I went to my room, I found that the mini-bar had several types of single malt Scotch in it. There was Budweiser--but no Miller--and lots of white wine. Hmm, exactly what I like—perfect. I went downstairs to the bar to meet some people for a drink. On the way I stopped off at the front desk and started a conversation with the lady working there. I asked her how they knew what I liked in my bar. She proceeded to tell me that, based on my last stay with them, they knew what drinks I bought the most and so on. This, in my opinion, is what makes the Ritz so dadgum special.

After her explanation, I asked her to tell me what she thought made the the Ritz so special. She said, "Well, we have a card we all carry in our pockets when we are working. The front of the card says, 'We are ladies and gentlemen serving ladies and gentlemen'. I think that sums it up well."

When I got to the bar to meet my friends, the bartender said, "Scotch and water, Mr. Beecham?" Are you kidding me? This was over the top. I felt invested in and special. Any place that puts my service at the top of their priority list will always get my business.

"We are ladies and gentlemen serving ladies and gentlemen." How profound! I don't have to think of myself as a lowly servant to others anymore. Nor should anyone think of me in that manner. The Ritz viewed me as more than a bottom line. To them I was an equal. The only real difference is that they had the opportunity to serve me.

We are all distinguished "ladies and gentlemen" serving one another, treating each other like real people with real lives. I didn't expect this kind of "human element" from a hotel but boy, was it refreshing. This is exactly the kind of mindset we need to have as bass-ackward business folk.

By keeping the helping without hustling mindset in all we do professionally, we can begin to develop ways to engage people that are both professional and human (yes, the two can be done simultaneously!). Our conversations stand as the entry point for developing authentic relationships with others. They are like little windows into the lives of others, so you need to know how to have one and how to make it go deeper than, "Hey, crazy weather we've been having."

The Power of Questions

One of the simplest ways to get to know someone is to ask them questions. The bass-ackward business approach is no different. In order to find out how you can help someone you must discover their needs. You have to get specific with your questions and be ready to act when the opportunity presents itself.

I learned to ask a stranger the same questions my mother would ask if I introduced one of my friends to her. I once met a guy named Boaz who encouraged me to always stay curious when talking with people. He said, "When you're having a conversation with someone, use natural curiosity to get deeper with them."

What I soon discovered was that most everyone has some kind of problem that I could help with. Usually these were problems that I could help solve simply by connecting them with someone else.

When you help without hustling you concentrate on the whole person not just the businessperson. Eventually, I found that I could

44

get business from anywhere. I didn't become one of those guys that only would talk to a "decision maker." No. I could get business from everybody.

Suddenly the receptionist and the garbage man became potential referral sources. I realized they knew people who owned houses. I discovered that if I helped them, they too would reciprocate. And it all stemmed from a basic conversation and me asking pointed questions.

Find The Pain

When you seek to discover the person and not the business opportunity he or she represents, you uncover pains you can alleviate or areas of expertise you can promote. When I followed this simple strategy, business started springing from the most unlikely sources.

The more questions you ask, the more you realize that almost everyone has something going on in their life that you can help with. My goal became to find out what it is! All you have to do is ask. If I spend enough time listening and focusing on you, I will eventually find a way.

I started looking for ways to help everyone. Now instead of cold calling on somebody, I was visiting with them and trying to help them figure out ways to grow their business. I was looking for ways that I could help them in their personal life. When I started doing this my life became so much more rewarding, and the great thing was people started helping me—an unexpected treat.

I quit trying to sell mortgages and myself; I just started looking for ways to serve others.

For example, consider the lady sitting next to you in the stands at the ballpark. While you are talking with her, go as deep into her life as she will let you. Try to find out what she really does at her job. Let's say she tells you that she's an account rep. I would ask questions like the following:

- Do you like your job?
- How long have you been doing that?
- What do you rep?
- Who do you call on?
- How do you grow your business?
- What would it take to get them?
- Who is a perfect customer for you?

You may know how to help her get that "perfect customer." You may know somebody who works for that company she wants to sell to. You may know her boss and can put in a good word for her. By asking questions like the ones above, you are on your way to getting down to the nitty-gritty of what makes this person tick.

Now all these questions are great, but the "perfect customer" question is the Holy Grail question. If you can get someone to tell you who their perfect customer is and then you deliver that perfect customer to their doorstep, you have officially "WOW'd" them.

If the same woman is a stay-at-home mom, find out what she is working on at home:

- What part of town do you live in?
- How do like your subdivision?
- Are you doing any projects around the house?
- Are the kids doing well in school?
- Did you have a career?
- Are you originally from here?
- Do you have to take care of family members?

She may mention that she is working on her yard or kitchen. Maybe she needs a plumber or a landscape architect. She may want to move out of her neighborhood and you could recommend a good real estate agent. Her kids may need some tutoring in school, sports or music. You might have a mutual friend from a different town. Are you getting the picture yet? YOU can help her!

I experienced a "baseball game conversation" once. While sitting in the stands watching my daughter Elyse's softball game, I struck up a conversation with the coach's wife. She explained to me that they were remodeling contractors. Several days later I met a woman who was looking to remodel her house and I remembered to give her the coach's name.

When I first met the coach's wife I asked her if she had an email address and phone number I could have; I then entered it into my database. After she received my email newsletter, she wanted to know if I could list them in my referral source area, which I gladly did. Several days later she had her favorite mortgage lady call me to talk about coming to work with us.

Say you're at a homeowners meeting—being the mayor of your village—and afterwards you strike up a conversation with one of the new neighbors. This is a perfect time to dig deep and discover something about them:

- Where did you live before ya'll moved here?
- What brought you to this town?
- What do you do for a living?
- How long have you been with your company?
- What do you do for them?
- So what do you spend most of your day doing?
- What do you do for fun?

He may tell you that he works in the accounting office of a major corporation or that he works on spreadsheets on the computer all day. You might not be able to help him there but he also told you his hobby is playing the guitar and you know some people who also like to play. Would he be excited if you took him to one of their picking sessions in another friend's basement?

Speaking of guitars and rocking out, let me tell you a quick story about Phil. My son Colin wanted to play guitar so I called my friend Phil, who has a guitar store. Phil connected me to a guy named Billy, who ended up giving Colin guitar lessons. It was a great connection! Billy was a great teacher and a tremendous inspiration to my son. But the story doesn't end there. It turns out that Billy and his wife were thinking of buying a lot in the mountains. "Beech, can you help us with that?"

"Of course I can."

So often the ways we can help people are so obvious and simple but for some reason we don't take that first step; for some reason we don't reach out to help our fellow man. I can't stress enough how important it is to be intentional in our conversations with people. By simply opening up our lives to people we invite them into our community; they benefit and so do we. This is called reciprocity and it is all but forgotten in our "me first" culture.

Don't Be Scared

My friends Ray and Rita introduced my wife and me to their friends Bill and Rhonda. As we were talking, I found out that they were interested in moving out of their subdivision and into some acreage, and had been looking for a while. I tried to ask as many questions as I could about why they hadn't found the right property yet.

Then several months later, my neighbor Arnold mentioned that he wanted to sell his house and acreage. I told Arnold to wait until Bill and Rhonda could see it. Long story short, they bought it. We have been neighbors and friends ever since.

As a result Bill asked me to do his loan and then sent me two other guys from his office for loans. What's more, Bill introduced me to the company that they worked for; this company handles all the sales for a whole area of condos—hundreds of sales per month! And guess who handles these loans?

Reciprocity! I sought to fulfill the needs of others and likewise, they returned the kindness. There's no bull here; just good old-fashioned care and consideration. Maybe it's the southerner in me—too much sweet tea, I guess. Whatever it is, I'm addicted to the feeling of helping others. I guarantee that once you start, you'll never stop.

If you are scared to meet new people then start by digging deeper with the ones you already know. You may generically know what "Bob" does but try to discover more about their job. "Hey, Bob ..."

- I know you're an account rep, but how do you get new customers?
- Are you looking for any new business?"
- What would your perfect customer look like?"
- What companies would you like to have?"

You may know someone that fits the profile.

Remember going on a date with someone you knew very little about? When you encounter someone new, think like you would on a blind date. Ask those kinds of questions. Try to figure out everything about them that you can. Be interested in knowing more about them. Use the blind date analogy when asking questions; things like:

- What do you do?

- How long have you been in that field?
- What is your favorite thing about your job?
- Tell me about your family. How many brothers and sisters do you have?
- Where did you go to school?
- Do you have any hobbies? What are they?

And the list goes on. Just think about the normal questions you would ask someone when you first meet them. But don't forget, be into the conversations and be genuinely interested in what the person has to say. This may mean that you have to put your own desires and agenda behind you just to hear this person's story. But once you know them and their story, you will know how you can help them. And that is the name of the game.

The more you do it the better you will become. Because the next time you see her at the ballpark, she will speak to you because you showed interest in her.

Case In Point

Hunter, one of my loan officers, wanted me to meet Greg Wohl, a condominium developer in downtown Atlanta. So I met with him. But instead of trying to sell him on my company, I tried to get to know him and his business better. I tried figuring out how I could help him. I started the meeting by asking Greg questions like:
- What kind of projects do you like to build?
- Where do you like to build?
- What makes your projects different?
- What do you do for fun?
- Are you single or married?

- What is your toughest challenge in developing projects?

Boom! The last one hit home. He answered, "Finding good locations. I want to be different. I'm an architect and I like artistic-looking projects. I want locations that will set me apart from my competition."

I told him about several properties that I knew were available but were not yet listed for sale. I suggested he go by and look at them. He agreed.

Now here is where the conversation goes to the next level. While I was drilling down with Greg, he told me that he was single and that he had a great appreciation for art. So I mentioned that I knew a young lady who shared his interest in art and recommended that he check her business website. He was a bit hesitant about the young lady until he got to her website and saw her picture. All of a sudden he was interested. So now I'm not only helping Greg with his business, I'm playing matchmaker!

To cap off our meeting I told Greg about a car show that was coming up. Why? Because while we were having our deep conversation, he had mentioned his love for collecting old cars. Because I drilled down with Greg and really got to know him I was able to connect him with things that might help his business, his personal life and his love life! If you want a holistic approach to business, you gotta be bass-ackward!

We parted ways with the understanding that he would let me know what he thought about the sites I mentioned. When we got out to the lobby, Hunter asked me why I didn't mention that we wanted to be one of his lenders. What do you think I told Hunter? I said, "Let's see what happens." Reciprocity takes a little bit of trust.

The next day he called, saying he was interested in both of the sites I suggested and that he wanted us to be his preferred lender on his next project. He also mentioned that he liked building long-term mutual relationships like we do.

Our goal was to be his preferred lender but that wasn't the driving force in our talks. Our first goal was to help him. We wanted to dig deep and discover a way to help him with one of his problems, not by asking him if we could be a preferred lender. Turns out that Greg valued what we, at my company, value: relationships.

The Real Reward

Anyone can make a good first impression but developing loyalty holds the real reward. Mark is consistently the top producer in my area and when we met, I applied a bass-ackward approach to our relationship. I quickly discovered that Mark loved riding dirt bikes with his son. This was something I knew much about since I love to ride too.

Our relationship began when I dug deep with him. He had some real estate in Florida and so did I. So I called him to talk to him about our properties in Florida and what he was doing with his since the economy was tanking. It was in that phone conversation that I found out about his affinity for riding dirt bikes.

"Man," I said, "we ride all the time. You should come on one of our rides." I was in the process of riding from Mexico to Canada in increments. So I took him and his son along on one of our rides and we developed a close relationship.

Then one day out of the blue Mark shows up at my door. "The company I was working for just shut down. Give me a desk, buddy." Man, what a blow! And what a blessing … all at once.

So here we are, years later, and Mark is my top salesman. Not only does he get the "helping without hustling" idea, he lives it every day. The guy is a monster in the industry. I'm fortunate to have him as part of my team.

The point here is that Mark and I were in the same industry doing the same thing, vying for the same business. And because I found out that we shared a common interest and didn't care that we were competitors, our relationship became deep. And who was the guy that Mark came to when he needed help? His friend … Beech.

Bass-Ackwards Nuts-n-Bolts

Here's how you discover someone's pain or expertise:

- Look for signs that signify pain. You're looking for a situation where somebody lets you know that they have something in life that isn't going well. If you ask someone, "How's your mom doing?" and they respond, "Ok," that's a sign that all is not well.
- Key: You have to discover the pain. You can't simply ask, "What's wrong?" If you do this then you've lost. No one will answer that question honestly. You must discover their pain through conversation.
- The reason you are digging deep is for you to discover things about the person. Simply asking them, "Betty, how can I help you in your business?" is a cop-out. You have to get to the bottom of their need by asking probing questions.
- To achieve the ultimate WOW factor in making connections, you must connect an expert in a certain area with someone who has a pain in that same field.

It seems that in this cutthroat type of society we are too guarded about friendships. Too often we cut ourselves off from relationships simply because we are greedy bastards. It may seem like a good idea but it cheapens our humanity. If I hadn't reached out to Mark and we hadn't gone on a few biking trips, we wouldn't have any memories, we wouldn't have a close relationship. People should always win over position or power.

Bass-Ackward Discoveries

In order to help someone you must dig deep and ask questions. The goal of your questions is to discover how you can best help that person. Maybe there is something serious they are dealing with. Find out what that pain is. Or maybe they have a unique expertise that you know would benefit someone else. Those are your goals: their pain and/or their expertise.

This all goes back to being emotionally involved with people and with the person you are talking to in particular. When you are emotionally involved with someone you remember things about them that you wouldn't otherwise. You remember their pains and pleasures—what makes them tick. So a good rule of thumb is to be all there in your conversations. Be into people.

When you make these grand discoveries about people you discover something even more startling and wonderful than just their pain and/or expertise. You discover them, as real people. You make a deep connection that will serve as the foundation for a lasting relationship.

***

54

In Chapter 5 we look at the next step after you've discovered someone's pain—how to alleviate it. It's one thing to ask questions for the sake of conversation, but it's another thing to move on what you've discovered. Most people do not expect the inquiry to go past idle banter at a baseball game. You, however, do not offer lip service. You are bass-ackward! Time to start putting actions to our words.

Chapter 5

Step Three: Alleviate Mr. Green's Pain

"Our problems are man-made, therefore they may be solved by man. No problem of human destiny is beyond human beings." —John F. Kennedy

Has anybody ever done an act of kindness for you? Didn't you just love it? Kindness has a way of easing so much tension and strife. You can be neck-deep in frustrating circumstances and all it takes is for someone to do something thoughtful for you and suddenly things don't seem that bad.

We all know what it's like to be on the receiving end of kindness. We know what it's like to receive timely help. But how many of us are looking to be the distributor of such kindness? How many of us are out there seeking ways to alleviate the pain of others?

I'm not just talking business circumstances either. I'm talking about helping someone through the toughness of life. This is what helping without hustling is all about: alleviating the pain of others.

It's digging deep to find someone's pain through authentic conversations and then doing something about it.

Lest you think I'm out to lunch on this concept, let me share with you a little conversation I had with a minister. One day I called our local pastor to see if he was interested in sitting on the board of an organization in the community. As we were talking, curiosity got the best of me so I asked, "Can I ask you a personal question?" "Sure," he replied. "What do most people want to talk about when they come up after a service to shake your hand—what do they say?" He thought for a moment then said, "Most people want to just say 'Hi,' to which I reply, 'How are you doing?' If they say, 'I'm doing ok' that is typically a pain signal." I was so intrigued!

He continued, "All you need is a thirty-second conversation to determine what their pain is and how I or the church can help them with their pain. Usually these pains aren't immediately solvable."

What the pastor is saying is that people want to talk to you about their pain; they just don't always verbalize it. But like the pastor said, after a few minutes of probing you can get right to the heart of the matter.

Family Struggle

Mr. Green, the local mechanic, came by my office one day to ask for my help (remember, I'm the mayor of my village). When his grandmother died, she left him some property, but here's where it gets tricky. The problem was that his step-cousins thought the land was theirs. All he knew was that she had told him it was part his. He wanted to know if I knew what to do about it.

Sure, I know what you're thinking. "Beech, you're no lawyer. You're not qualified to do that." And you're right. But when you're the go-to guy or gal you find ways to help people. There's always someone who is qualified to help; it's your job as mayor of your village to know who that person is. In this case, I didn't need to look too far.

I asked him to give me the address of the property and to give me his full name and the full names of everyone in his family. I needed a family tree for as far as he could remember. He wrote it down and I told him I would have my attorney check the title of the property.

He wanted to know what it cost. I told him it wouldn't cost anything. I knew that I sent the attorney plenty of business; title research was something they could do very easily. However, if the property in question ended up to be his, I thought it would be fair to pay him for his time. He agreed.

Several days later I arranged a meeting between him and the attorney. It appeared he did, in fact, have legal claim to the property. He thought he was out of luck since the cousins had been living on the property for many years. So, that was that, right?

Fast forward one year later. I'm sitting at my favorite local diner and guess who walks up to me with the best news? You got it: Mr. Green. He tells me how much he appreciated me helping him because it looked like he was going to get some money for the property! I told him it couldn't have happened to a nicer guy.

I tell you this story to show you that when you make yourself open and available to help others, great things happen. The by-product of helping Mr. Green is that I became a preferred customer for life. I may not have received a ton of business from helping Mr. Green but I did land on his radar. But more importantly, I received psychic income from helping Mr. Green. We'll talk more on this in the coming pages.

If ever I need some mechanic work done, I know where to go. What's more, I now have someone I know and trust to refer to others who may need some help with their cars. Again, in this situation is the element of trust. When he was in real need, I made a couple of phone calls and helped him. I wasn't leveraging a position, nor did I help with that intent. A great local man needed some help, so I obliged.

We put too much emphasis on pressuring people to do things we want in order to make a quick buck. The truth is if you start caring for people by alleviating some pain in their lives, you've just given them the best sales pitch money can buy. They don't teach *that* in MBA programs!

You: The Natural Resource

In order to be able to help people you must become one of your community's natural resources. No, I don't mean like water or fuel. I mean you must become someone others look to in order to find solutions to their problems. After I started having deep conversations with people, word got out that I was a great resource for helping people.

I started getting phone calls from people who needed help in solving large and small problems. Most of the problems had nothing to do with my business, but the more people I helped the more contacts I made. I estimate that 25% of the phone calls I take every day are to help someone with something other than mortgages. Wouldn't you rather help someone than make a bunch of cold calls all day? Me too.

I love helping people; that's why I got into the mortgage business in the first place. Every time I help someone I have a new contact. So each time I help someone I am exponentially growing my company—and I feel great doing it. Once the contacts start coming in, I use my simple formula to keep track of everyone. If you do things the bass-ackward way then you must be all about service. Not just helping people in need but going the extra mile for them when and if they do become a client. You don't help someone with a smile and a kind gesture only to treat them a different way as a client.

This means you must be intentional about how you keep track of the people in your sphere of influence. Remember, they are no longer just contacts. They are real people who trust you—many consider you a true friend. What an awesome responsibility. Now seize that responsibility by doing your due diligence; develop a simple way to keep track of them bass-ackward style (more on this at the end of the chapter).

Service Sells

As my business grew I received "Top Gun" awards from the Georgia Association of Mortgage Brokers for high personal production and corporate loan volume. I served on the board and was elected president of the Georgia Mortgage Brokers Association. Many of my peers started seeking out my advice. In 2001 I was one of the top loan officers in the country, according to Broker Magazine.

I don't include these accolades to puff myself up. I include them to show you that helping people is not an empty endeavor. Will you find results similar to mine? Not necessarily, but you might. You will, however, find a reward that is arguably of greater value than material assets and performance awards.

Allow me to talk straight to you for a minute. These principles we are discussing don't necessarily come easy for men. We generally like to fumble around with our words and talk sports and weather and liquor. Women, however, tend to get this easier.

Now don't go waving your "Beech is a male chauvinist!" flag, because I'm not. I think both sexes are uniquely geared for specific things. That's the beauty of humanity. Women tend to understand the nurturing elements of helping without hustling better than men—and they are better at it.

Maybe you're a woman who just cannot stand cold calling. It's just not in you to do well using that method for sales. But imagine if you spent some time calling a few business relationships with the mindset and message that you wanted to help them grow their business. This mindset alone puts you in a different place mentally. Already you are seeking to serve and it feels good; it feels like you are nurturing an associate and their business.

Now don't get me wrong. Men can still do this kind of thing; we are just much slower on the draw than women. I better quit while I'm ahead here, eh?

Getting back to it…Being a great resource for others allowed me to gain "psychic income." Psychic income describes compensation that's more important than money—it's something you feel; it gives you deep personal worth. An example of this concept involved Adele, a Jamaican immigrant, whose car got a flat right outside my office one day. Traffic didn't even slow, so she was in harm's way and couldn't get the car to the side of the road.

I walked out to see if I could help and noticed that she was flustered and didn't know what to do. The cops showed up and told her she had to have it towed but Adele couldn't afford it. Something had to give.

Without thinking, I told the police to call the tow truck and that I would take care of the towing fee. Adele instantly relaxes. When the whole ordeal finally settles down and the tow truck shows up, Adele thanks me for my help. I slipped her a hundred dollar bill and wished her well. "I know today's been very rough on you. Please take this to help with your expenses," I said.

Adele was stunned and began to cry. Her gratitude touched me deeply, as we both felt a bond develop through this very trying situation. A few weeks later a tall, well-built man comes to the front door of our building and asks to see me (gulp). I walk out and the man says, "My wife told me that you are the man that helped her out a few weeks ago. I just wanted to tell you how much I respect you for helping her and treating her well. Thank you." We chatted a bit and he left.

That is what psychic income is. That feeling or bond or butterfly in your soul that gives you a transcendent peace. In your mind you say, "Ah. Now that felt good. That's what life is all about."

Defining Reciprocity

Being a great resource for others results in reciprocity from others. Roger Wise talks about this concept in a story he shared with me:

To: Steve Beecham
From: Roger Wise, Jr.
Re: Service Sells

Steve,
It was our responsibility to call on and sell to the Children's Medical Service Clinics and present to them our product lines. In a clinic, through conversation

with the supervisor, it was brought to my attention that the state funding for this program was inadequate; therefore they had to set up waiting lists of children, in particular those patients awaiting surgery. The clinic supervisor had three such patients: A decision had to be made on who would get surgery and who would not get surgery.

There were only enough funds in the budget for two surgical procedures. There was a lot of concern that the baby not receiving immediate surgery would die before the funds were made available. Steve, I came back to Atlanta and contacted the Chairman of the House Appropriations Committee and the Senate Appropriations Committee. I persuaded them that we should have hearings on this issue and present adequate funding for this program.

The Speaker of the House called a special meeting in his conference room with the understanding that three million dollars was needed to appropriately fund the Children's Medical Service Programs.

The day arrived and the usual players were there: state program people, doctors, administrators, and lobbyists. They gave their opinions, but the most important comments came from the clinic supervisor who woke at 3:00 a.m. to make the five-hour drive to Atlanta. Those comments presented the facts. They were so compelling that the Speaker asked the

Chairman of the House Appropriations Committee, "Can you find three million dollars to adequately fund this program and do away with the waiting list?" He advised that he could.

He then turned to the Chairman of the Senate Appropriations Committee and asked, "If we put it in the budget, will you keep it in the budget?" He stated that he would. The Speaker then said, "We have done the right thing. We have done away with the waiting list. This meeting is adjourned."

Steve, you wouldn't believe it. The word got out that me and my company were helpful allies beyond all expectations in these matters. That year our district was number one in the nation in all product lines sold to the Children's Medical Service Clinics throughout our state. You are right. There is no substitute for doing the right thing and serving others. Service sells.

Learning Reciprocity

The art of reciprocity is not necessarily something we are born with but we do learn it at an early age. Robert Cialdini says that reciprocity is found in every society in the world. We are taught to be nice to others and say, "Yes, sir," and "No, ma'am." We're instructed by our parents to help our friends, neighbors and family. When someone offers you something you say, "Thank you." When you lend a helping hand to your friend, they are more likely to return the favor.

As it was in our youth, so it is in the professional business realm. You can (re)learn and apply these skills to improve your business. It is a known sales fact that people prefer to do business with people they like. You always like those who show interest in you. But it's not just about going to a seminar that will help you learn how to deal better with people; it's about adopting a lifestyle that puts others first. It's about maintaining a mindset that seeks to help others.

There are a lot of people, including me, who believe it really is deeper than being liked. Many people believe that love is the driving force in all things we do. We do a lot of things because we want people to love us. If you feel the love of another individual then you will go to war for them.

I know this concept may seem odd being discussed in what is essentially a business book, but I hope you realize by now that bass-ackward business is bass-ackward because it's not solely about business. It's about a lifestyle that values people. It's about a business mentality that does not shy from words like trust and love. Do your customers feel your love?

Based on these bass-ackward concepts, I have made it my mission to do the right thing. The right thing is helping others first and showing your fellow man that you care. I want to learn as much about you as I can. The more I know, the more I can help. My breakthrough was realizing that when you apply these personal values to sales, it's amazing how easy it is to sell.

You Get What You Give

I have recently come to know Ron Clark. Ron won the Teacher of the Year award several years ago and wrote a best-selling book. He has been on Oprah twice! They even made a movie about him. Why?

Because Ron has proven that if your students know you really care about them, they will perform for you.

You see, Ron took the worst kids in Harlem and made them the highest scoring students in the school. He spent time getting to know the kids and their home lives. He jumped rope with the girls on the playground and attended one student's baseball games on Saturdays. The kids began to believe that Ron really cared about them. Once this trust was established, the kids began to perform for him in the class-room.

Now, I met Ron at the Rotary Club one day. My buddy Roger comes up to me and says, "Hey Beech, I want you to meet someone. This is Ron Clark." So I said, "Oh, you look familiar to me." My buddy Roger said, "Well, Beech, that's probably because he's been on Oprah twice and written a best-selling book."

So I shook Ron's hand and told him, "Now I know why you look so familiar to me. You're the guy that's been sleeping with my wife." Completely shocked, he replied, "Excuse me?" "Yeah, my wife has been reading your book each night before she goes to sleep. She's nuts about what you're doing."

Relieved, Ron laughs while I call my wife right then and there. "Honey, guess who I'm talking to right now." "Who?" "Ron Clark!" She goes bonkers, "Oh my gosh, Ron Clark … " You get the picture. It was a fun first meeting.

I then said to Ron, "Hey, Ron, whenever you're ready to start making some real money with this book, just let me know." Rotary Clubs are great and he could sell books for $20 a pop. But he needed funding for his school and he wasn't going to get there in $20 chunks. "I'm all ears," he said.

So we talked after his speech and I told him I could throw a party for him where people could not only pick up his book, but also find out what he was doing with his school. And the people at this party would be the kind of people who would lay down the $20 for the book and then write out a nice check to support the school.

The party was a huge success and Ron was hooked. "How can we set up more of these?" he asked. It's all about making the connection, going deep and filling a need.

So there are two takeaways from Ron's story:

1. Ron understood the value of helping others. He took a personal interest in the whole student; their school life and their family life. He built trust in a community and saw amazing results. The application for us: if you go to one of your customer's kid's baseball games do you think they would notice? You better believe it! Would they think you care about them? Absolutely! I have come to believe this is true for anybody.

2. When meeting Ron Clark, I wasted no time seeing how I might help him and his cause. He's doing a great work in the lives of these children and in the community. My always-growing sphere of influence allowed me to fill a need that Ron had: raising money for his school.

The Ron Clark illustration shows us that if we are truly vested in the lives of others we can make a difference. Also, if we are diligent in growing our sphere of influence it not only becomes a network for future business, but it becomes a tool to help and celebrate the common good for the whole community.

●

Bass-Ackward Relief

So what do you do once you start a conversation with someone? You're on your way to getting through to them with some thoughtful questions and then it surfaces. You realize that this person has a need that you can fill—they have some pain that you can alleviate. Great! Now don't just shake your head and act empathetic to their situation. Become an activator.

When you take the time to make a phone call for someone or look into a matter yourself or connect someone in need with someone who can fill that need, you become a human resource. It's all about getting to the heart of the matter with each person you come in contact with.

Ask good questions. Find their pain. Alleviate it. You'll be glad you did.

Bass-Ackward Nuts-n-Bolts

Here's your hotlist for discovering and helping with someone's pain:

- **Lead The Horse:** Helping someone alleviate pain is like leading a horse to water; it doesn't have to be something you do personally, but maybe you point them in the direction of a great group that can help with their particular pain/pleasure.
- **Acts of Kindness:** Helping a complete stranger also helps build the idea of reciprocity.
- **Psychic Income:** Sometimes when you help someone

> alleviate pain you receive psychic income instead of real
> income, which will bring you more joy in the long run.
> • **Reciprocity:** When you help someone alleviate their
>   pain, it creates a "WOW" with them, which puts them
>   in a place of wanting to reciprocate.

***

In the next chapter we'll discover that sometimes people don't have specific areas of pain or need in their lives. But what they do have is an area of expertise that sets them apart from other people. The problem is no one knows them. What does that mean for you? Now you go from pain alleviator to expertise promoter. Not only is it fun to celebrate the expertise of others; it's bass-ackward!

Chapter 6

Step Four: Promote Joe's Expertise

"All lasting business is built on friendship."
—Alfred A. Montapert

Sometimes you get into conversations and find that people don't want to get into their pains or personal lives. But this is not a closed door—it's a great opportunity. You can use the conversation to delve into their areas of expertise; their hobbies, their passions; all the things that make them want to get up in the morning.

As knowing someone's pain allows you to know how to help them, knowing someone's expertise allows you to better promote them. When you know what someone is good at, you can use them as a resource to help solve other people's problems. Plug them into your network and you become their promoter.

I discovered, as I asked people about their lives, that everyone is an expert in some field or has special knowledge about something they are passionate about. When I discovered a person's passion, it opened up a whole new world. They started to glow as they told me

71

about their favorite subject. The conversation would always take on new meaning and direction.

I now make a special effort to find my new friends' favorite passions because if they are passionate about it, then they are usually an expert about it.

For example, my friends Chad and Todd had recently collaborated to form a new Internet company. I ran into them one day and asked them all about it. Through the course of our conversation I asked them what, exactly, their new company did. They invited me over to the office to see a PowerPoint presentation.

During the presentation they mentioned that they thought a particular major company was interested in using them as a subcontractor. When they said the name of the company I remembered that Cynthia, a real estate agent friend of mine, had a daughter, Alexis, that worked for this company. ("Connect the dots and promote someone's expertise!" I thought.)

As I thought about their situation I remembered that Alexis had a senior-level position with this company in the northeast. So I got into my activator role. I called Cynthia to get Alexis' cell phone number. Since it was during the Christmas break it just so happened that she was in town for the holidays!

After we talked briefly on the phone, Alexis decided to come over and talk to Chad and Todd—right then and there. As of this writing it appears she loved what they were doing so much that she went to work with them. Not only will she be able to sell back to her old company, but she'll also be able sell to some new companies Chad and Todd had not even thought about.

Connect The Dots

I could end this chapter right here with that illustration alone. Don't worry; I have more. Let's take a second and connect the dots here. Very simple:

- After entering a conversation that was focused on what Chad and Todd were doing, their new endeavor surfaced (as expected).
- I went one step further and took a genuine interest in this new venture that I knew very little about.
- After probing a little more—this time on a more professional level—I found a need that I could fill: big client connection.
- I didn't lollygag around. I called my contact on the spot and took advantage of the situation on behalf of Chad and Todd.
- The call to Cynthia's daughter was me "promoting Chad and Todd's expertise." And it worked.
- The main point of the story is that a great connection was made that might never have been if I didn't start a conversation. A need was filled; an expertise was promoted.
- The bonus: Alexis moved back to Atlanta to work for Chad and Todd, which put her back near her family. Alexis, being a single mom and moving back home, made Cynthia a happy camper as well. Everyone made out on the connection! Perfect.

Here's another example of how all this works in real life:

I got a call from my banker, Ross. He told me that he was on a committee to get Casey Cagle elected as Lt. Governor of Georgia. They needed a place to host a cocktail party and wanted to know

73

if I would do it at my house. My wife Mary agreed and so we did. Casey won the election!

Several weeks later I called Casey to see if he would meet with Ron Clark. He agreed. Hopefully they can help each other and the kids in Georgia. It all started by hosting a political function at my house. Since I've met both Casey and Ron, they have referred business back to me. A simple gesture to connect others can often lead to the opportunity to grow your business.

One connection leads to another, leads to another. And it all begins with being open to helping others when the opportunity comes up.

My Revelation

I learned that knowing my friends' expertise and passion became critically important when I was trying to help other people. It became apparent that these two elements of the bass-ackward way were in-extricably linked. The best way to help someone is to connect that person with someone who is an expert in the area of their problem.

So, my job became connecting one friend's need with another's expertise. The reality became clear that by helping one friend solve a problem, I was helping another friend increase his business.

Most highly successful people work in the area of their passion. If you know a local photographer and you meet somebody thinking about buying a camera, then wouldn't it make sense to introduce them? Your friend gets advice from an expert and the expert meets someone who could potentially send them more customers.

The Dark Horse

I tried out my newest revelation recently, in a local mayor's race. My friend Joe entered the contest as a dark horse so I decided to help him. Part of my strategy was to convince people he could win. I started telling people he was going to win because "Beech was on his team." I spread the word through my large local network (aka my "sphere of influence") that I was on Joe's team. Now come on, cut me some slack. It was definitely too "braggy" for me but it was the only thing I could come up with at the moment.

The strange thing is that it caught on! Twenty-three days later someone came up to me at a party and said, "I understand Joe is going to win because you are on his team." Let's take a step back here before we get to the end of the story. There are few things at play here. First and most obvious is that I am seeking to help my friend fulfill his dream. I will argue that I was also helping to fill a need: victory.

Second, I got right to work at promoting Joe's expertise and credentials. I was shameless in my promotion, which worked partly because it was me—"Beech, the straight shooter." But it also worked because I was already established in my community as the go-to guy—the mayor, if you will. I knew a lot of people who trusted me and would get behind something if I dove in headfirst. Well, I dove and they followed.

Lastly, there is also an element of "buzz" going on in this scenario. By essentially becoming Joe's "street team" I was instrumental at creating "buzz." I don't have to tell you that buzz is when people talk about you and or your product.

Buzz is what people say after something: "Man, that party was great. Joe seems like a great guy—awesome family." Creating buzz sounds like:

"Hey, do you know John?"

"No, I don't."

"Well, John is the new dentist in town and I hear he can get teeth whiter than anybody."

John's buzz is his ability to get teeth white. What is your buzz? What do people say about you? Buzz was at work in Joe's candidacy; people talking turned to people voting.

Well, he pulled it off. He won and some people think it is because of me. But the main point here is that I was active in promoting Joe's expertise to be mayor and had a small part in helping him succeed.

Is there buzz around town about you and your business? If not, ask yourself why not. It's probably because you aren't actively seeking to help people. Remember, people will talk when someone is shaking things up. You do that by being bass-ackward.

Bass-Ackward Promotion

What is better than self-promotion? Promoting others. As part of the helping without hustling mindset, promoting the expertise of others in part and parcel to alleviating someone's pain or filling a need.

In this chapter we've looked at examples of how a simple conversation can lead to the realization that to help this person, all you have to do is basically connect the dots. But promoting a friend's expertise is only possible if you've spent time building your personal network—filling your database with people who each have something to offer.

I mentioned earlier that I could create buzz for my friend's election because I had worked hard to become the mayor of my village. People knew I was trustworthy and that I would reciprocate a referral if I received one. So you see, you can't just assert yourself in a space where you haven't earned the right to promote someone. There is a system to all of this, if you haven't noticed. But the thing is, it's not about the system; it's about helping others.

Too many people get locked into to a system. If this is you, be careful. The net result of systematizing relationships is that you lose social equity. You forfeit solid relationships for the opportunity to leverage people. This is not the bass-ackward way. This is just plain wrong. It might get you so far, but I've found that nothing will deepen your impact on your community better than investing in the lives of people.

When I mention "system," I am merely trying to get you to make sure you keep track of the people you come in contact with. It matters to people if you remember them. It matters to people if you care enough to call them with the opportunity to use their expertise to help someone out and earn some business. So be intentional about how you treat the valuable resource that is the lives of others.

Quick review: while you're drilling deep with someone, be cognizant of their unique talent or ability or expertise. You never know when the dots will connect for you in a conversation. And when they do, don't hesitate. Connect them! Make the call. Create the relationship. Help out a friend. It's like playing Lite Brite as a kid! As you put those little glow things on the black board, a beautiful picture forms. It glows. It's beautiful. It's bass-ackward.

Bass-Ackward Nuts-n-Bolts

I have a little saying (well, I have a lot of "little sayings") that goes like this: "Whoever meets the most people wins!"

You need to put yourself in a position to meet new people so that you can promote their area of expertise. What does that look like?

- Join clubs: Rotary clubs, library clubs, chess clubs ... you name it
- Visit with your friends and neighbors unexpectedly whenever you have the chance
- Get involved with political groups—help your local mayor get re-elected, etc.
- Volunteer with a non-profit. Not only does this connect with people of like minds, but it lets you give back to the community. It gives you a tremendous amount of psychic income and brings joy to your heart.
- When you join up with one of these groups, get dialed in with a subgroup within the larger group. This will allow you to know more people personally and drill deep with individuals on a regular basis. As you get to know these people, they will in turn introduce you to their friends.

***

In the next chapter we are going to wrap up the bass-ackward idea and touch on a few more practical ways to live it out. These ideas are not complicated. They do, however, require you to be authentic with your fellow man and to be diligent in keeping track of your relationships. It's all about being in the moment and connecting with people whenever you can.

Chapter 7

Embracing the Bass-Ackward Way

"The people who know you and love and care about
you want you to be successful; they just don't know
how."
–Steve Beecham

Helping others is good for your health. This phenomenon is called the "helper's high" ("Helper's high" is the term coined by Arizona State University psychologist Robert Cialdini in his research to describe the euphoria reported by frequent givers). It is often followed by feelings of increased self worth, calm, and relaxation. Nearly 80% of those surveyed reported that the good feelings would return, though in diminished intensity, when the helping act was remembered. Nine out of ten felt that they were healthier than others of their age group. Volunteers who later on get to see and witness the personal reactions of the person they are helping are more likely to report helper's high, increased self-esteem, and reduced signs of stress.

What does this mean? That helping is good for you! That if we make helping others a common occurrence in our lives—even the norm for our lives—then we benefit physically and emotionally from it.

It helps us emotionally because it provides us with a healthy distraction from the everyday happenings that tend to be completely self-focused. Focusing on others takes us away, at least temporarily, from the hassles of work, finances, or family troubles.

Let's not ignore the fact that we get a special kind of attention from those we help. It makes us feel that we matter to someone. Helping can also block pain because our attention is shifted from personal pain to helping others. Helping others improves our outlook and enhances our sense of gratitude for what we have.

The Rubber Meets The Road

Have I convinced you that helping others is the best way to grow your business? Have I convinced you that helping others is actually a healthy habit to adopt? Are you beginning to see the value in initiating deep conversations with the people you run into every day? I hope you have picked up a nugget or two in this short book that will help you gain the confidence you need to be bass-ackward in your business approach. I hope that you will see the value in helping people with no strings attached.

I know it is a bit of a faith leap. "Beech, you want me to stop making cold calls and just help people and build up my contacts and spend all my time serving that contact list. You want me to look for daily opportunities to help others first and to promote the experts on my list? But what about me? I've got to make a living!"

Believe me, I get it. It's not easy giving up an approach that seems to provide results—namely a steady income. But look past the immediate. Look to where you want to be with your business and your personal life. What will bring you true fulfillment? I guarantee you that if you begin helping others you will see a massive change in your own life. Not only will you begin to see how your efforts affect others, but you will find that your life comes into focus—things are clearer. You have found worth in something that seems to always be giving worth away. That's the beauty of helping without hustling!

So start having fun in your work by making someone else's day. Go looking for it. Quit cold calling people with the idea of selling them something. Call them with idea of helping them. The next time you run into someone and initiate a conversation find out what their expertise is—watch them glow as they talk about it.

A guy named Danny Thomas once said, "All of us are born with a reason, but all of us don't discover why. Success in life has nothing to do with what you gain in life or accomplish for yourself. It's what you do for others." So many of us, especially those of us in business for ourselves, think that success is equated with our bottom line. We think that we are measured as people by the things we accumulate or how fat our 401(k)s are. But this just ain't true.

Our business life should be an extension of who we are as human beings—real people. When people encounter us out and about in the community, who do they find? Are we people who are eager to know how they are doing in their lives and work? Or do we just see dollar signs and opportunities? Our purpose in life isn't just to collect everything we can and die. Those of us who discover that life is about helping others find the riches that come from that, while those of us who are just out to better ourselves usually lead lonely, empty lives.

George Washington Carver said, "How far you go in life depends on your being tender with the young, compassionate with the aged, sympathetic with the striving, and tolerant of the weak and strong. Because some day in life you will have been all of these." Success in

81

life can only be gained when our perspective starts inward—"How would I want to be treated as an individual?" If this is our starting point then we will deal fairly with our friends and our clients.

A Final Word

Wouldn't boosting your customer base be simpler if all it required was getting to know the people who cross your path and then finding ways to help them? This is the bass-ackward way! When you adopt it for yourself, you are agreeing to get out more and always engage the people before you. You are agreeing to become a full-time helper, to always look for opportunities to serve others, not hustle them for business. You are agreeing to enter conversations and the relationships they initiate with a simple trust in the good nature of people to remember those who helped them.

No matter who you are you can enrich your life and the lives of others through service. All the people you meet have problems just like you do. You can turn normal conversations into something that really helps people when they need it. I know of no better way to spread your influence!

It is a trustworthy, noble strategy. Best of all, it works because "Goodness," as Thoreau put it, "is the only investment that never fails."

Epilogue

Bass-ackward Words From Bass-ackwards Friends

I have so many great friends and colleagues who now use the principles of the Bass-Ackward Way. Some of them were skeptics; others were early adopters. The main thread with them all is that this approach to business is legit. Not only have these principles helped them find success in business, but their lives have been enhanced as well. Here are a few kind words from a few great friends.

Handing Out Cash

Dan Merkel
Sr. Account Executive
Southern States Insurance

Steve first confided in me his approach to doing business about two years ago. I was intrigued to say the least because I was cranking out business the old fashioned way: one phone call at a time, one meeting to explain what I do at a time, one "elevator speech" at a time and one request to do business at a time.

It was dulling to say the least and I was not

having any fun. Not long after this I made a change and joined a firm much closer to my house with a mindset of doing business different. This was my opportunity to start over and incorporate the principals Steve was using in his business.

My wife trusted me but my coworkers looked at me like I had three eyes. The first "traditional" sales meeting at my new firm was interesting. I was asked to share my top 10 prospects and where they came from. I responded that I did not have any prospects "so to speak." I had three deals working at the time and they asked, "What do you think your chances are of closing these deals?" I responded 100%. No doubt this came across a bit cocky from the new guy but I explained how I was operating.

The three deals were calls from different business owners who said similar things. So and so gave me your name and said you are the man for insurance. Each deal had a tie back to someone I had either helped with a problem or made considerable effort to help (i.e., one gentleman was out of work and I put him in front of several people who helped him network and get a job. He got a job and then called to ask if I would handle the insurance at his new company.)

My efforts and sincerity closed all three deals. Not my "value added list" or my ability to out talk my competitor. (Note: I have an advanced designation in insurance so I really do know what I am doing when they do come to me).

Here I am one year later and I was one of the top three producers last year and I am on track to have another great year. I sum it up for people when I say: "Given a choice, would you rather walk down Main Street every day and ask everyone you see for a $20 bill or walk down Main Street every day and hand out $20 bills?" What sounds like more fun, begging or giving?

With this program giving wins every time. I am having a blast. Thanks Steve.

From Cold Calling Specialist To Bass-Ackward

Ira Jolley

Commercial Insurance Agent

W.S. Pharr & Company

When I first met Steve a few years ago, I was a Sales Manager at AT&T Wireless Services. I was taught to teach my sales teams the "old school" sales prospecting methods of cold calling, which was done at AT&T for years and years. We were told that this was the "best" way to make the numbers, so that is how we taught our reps. We were made to hold them accountable to prospecting numbers which revolved on hundreds of cold calls made per month.

I remember Steve telling me how this was not the way to achieve high goals and that you have to get to know the people on a personal level if you really

87

wanted to be successful. For years, he would tell me this, and for years I continued to be a huge proponent of cold calling. I thought I was pretty successful doing it this way, so why change?

About 4 years ago, I left the telecom industry after a 16-year career to pursue a new endeavor into the Commercial Property Insurance world. In my first year as a P&C (W.S. Pharr & Company) Commercial Agent, I was convinced that I could become a top producer using all the cold calling techniques I was accustomed to using. I was able to get a great deal of appointments and proposals out the door. I quickly learned, however, that my prospective clients preferred to work with someone they knew because they had a relationship built, or because they were referred to them by a trusted source.

Steve continued to help mentor me in his referral and networking techniques for building solid business and personal relationships. I now NEVER make any cold calls, and I am quickly building a solid book of business through my referral and networking activities.

Thanks Beech for helping me work smarter, enjoy what I do, and build a great book of business while helping my own network of people in the process!

Gearing Up To Help

Scott French
Office and Retail Leasing Specialist

Beech and I have been friends for a long time. We have always worked on helping each other figure out ways to improve our business. Over the years I have come to understand that my marketing methods while in the custom jewelry business were for the most part a gamble that never seemed to pay off. So I just did not do it.

My small jewelry business survived and I made a reasonable income, but I never really thrived. In hindsight, the reason for this would be that I didn't fully implement all of Steve's steps. I did always have the idea of helping others, but I did not go far enough with the database management and the regular contacts.

Since my transition from the jewelry business to the commercial real estate business, I have paid more attention to Beech's ideals and have worked hard at applying them. It's not the easiest thing in the world to do but the rewards are amazing.

In commercial real estate, relationships are everything. I now have a myriad of opportunities to help others solve many different problems. Beech is right; by helping others solve problems I, in turn, build relationships. I work hard on adding everyone that I meet to my database along with notes about them,

89

what they do, how I met them and how I may be able to help. I refer back to these notes on a regular basis so that the needs of others are always fresh in my mind.

In real estate, many agents have the notion that "dialing for dollars" is the only way to get new business. By now the average agent would have made thousands of cold call by now. But I have not made more than one hundred. My business is steadily growing, in spite of one of the worst real estate cycles in history.

Why my success? Because I believe in trying hard to solve problems for folks without asking "What's in it for me?" If what Beech says is true about staying in constant contact with my database and if I can gear up for that ... I may not be able to keep up!

Epilogue

Appendix

Some Final Bass-Ackward Nuts-n-Bolts

Welcome to my "appendix." Here you'll find some extra tidbits that will help you apply the bass-ackward way to your business.

Bass-Ackward Referrals

Ok, so you've heard me talk a lot about referrals or "my referral list." This list is so important. It's a list you need to build from your contact list. This list will be the one you go to when someone calls or emails you with a real-life need. For me, being in the mortgage industry, this list largely relates to housing problems. I do, however, keep other referral numbers on my list, like mechanics, private schools, or even the best gym in the area.

So, let's make your list. Here are the categories I'd include on my list. Check it out and then retrofit your list for your particular industry:

Referral List Categories:

- Plumbers
- Electricians
- Carpenters
- Roofers
- Landscapers
- Teachers
- Attorneys
- Accountants
- Real Estate Agents
- Travel Agents
- Private Schools

I think you get the idea. If you start filling these categories with reputable names, then you will have a great tool for helping others. If you know some of these off the top of your head, put them on the list. If you don't have any of these, take some time at the end of the workday to call people you know to fill in the list. Here's what you do:

- Ask others for referrals.
- Then call the referral.
- Tell the service provider what you are doing and that they will get business from your referrals.
- Give your customer the referral and tell them to mention your name when they contact the contractor.
- Don't be afraid to give out more than one name. The more people who know you are trying to help, the better. This way the customer gets to decide which one they like best.
- Then publish this list on your web page and newsletter. This

lets people know that you know a lot of people.

Referrals end up serving as your personal ad, so be sure you are living up to the buzz created by the person who is referring you to others. You can do this through honest messaging on your newsletter or in a mission statement found on your website. When people are referred to someone the first thing they do is look them up on the Internet. What are others saying of this person? Does it match their own messaging? Make sure you are being honest in what you say and what people can easily find out about you.

When people begin passing the word around that you are a straight shooter, your buzz takes on a life of its own. Pretty soon people will naturally come to you as "the go-to guy or gal" because they know you are trustworthy and actually care about people. This is when you know the bass-ackward way is in full effect.

When you get a call from a referral remember to:

- Ask how they found you. "Who gave you my name?" Be winsome and conversational about this. Don't be stiff and business-like.
- When they tell you, make a note of this and set up a system to thank that person for the referral. (I always thank my referral even if I don't get the deal or make money on the deal.)
- Find out is how they know the referral source. This establishes rapport.
- Then talk about things unrelated to business. Get to know a little about them.
- After some conversation I then start down the road of the real reason they called.
- Look for ways to refer them to your friends. For example, if

95

they are moving into a new house they may need a good termite guy or painter, etc. If they do, I refer them out. By providing more service you add more value to their situation. You have now become a one-stop-shop to this person.

- Don't underestimate the power of sending other people business. Be their sales force. Help them grow their business and they will help you.

Bass-Ackward Newsletter

What do we do with contacts once we get them. Of course you want to be a good steward of your relationships, so you need to have a plan.

I keep track of my new contacts in a database. I then stay in constant contact with them through my weekly newsletter. My contacts hear from me every week—52 times a year. But don't just make a ho-hum newsletter. Some helpful tips:

- Your newsletter needs to be like a People Magazine not like a Fortune Magazine. Why? Because People Magazine is a fun magazine about other people who are doing interesting things. A Fortune Magazine is all about you and how to make your business better. You want people to read your newsletter and enjoy it, not delete it. You want people to be able to connect with others through it. So make your newsletter about your customers and their lives and businesses. Not about you and yours.

- Make it an extension of your new helping without hustling mindset. Have a place where people can post "needs" and make it easy for others to contact with those people to fill those needs. Use it as a tool to connect people of expertise with people in need.

- Promote businesses others can connect with. Promote someone's resume who may be in need of work. Promote rental property if they need help getting tenants.

Here are a couple of important notes about meetings.

- Do coffee, not lunch. Brian Hilliard says coffee is not as big a commitment as lunch. Coffee allows the other party to leave after a few minutes if the conversation is not of interest.
- Always try to meet near your target's office or home so that their time commitment is less. If things go well they may be willing to stay longer or to set up a subsequent meeting where you can talk more in depth.

About Steve Beecham

Steve Beecham has become "the Mayor of his village." As a successful Atlanta area businessman and entrepreneur, he has spent many years seeking the perfect scenario: "My phone rings and people ask to spend money with me."

He has owned a mortgage company, a retail store, a garbage business and rental real estate . Steve is past president of the Georgia Association of Mortgage Brokers, and has been listed as one of the Top 5 loan officers and Top 5 mortgage companies in the state of Georgia by the Atlanta Business Chronicle.

Devoting himself to reading and studying the behavior of others, Steve has interviewed hundreds of top salespeople to identify the common elements of success. Through trial and error, he developed his remarkable system of helping people but not hustling them for business. As President of Home Town Mortgage, he has taught his strategies to the people that work there , with amazing results. "Bass-Ackward Business" has helped him recruit and retain the top mortgage people in the area.

Steve has served on the boards of numerous nonprofits and has led the way in proposing innovative marketing ideas to help them grow their businesses. He has for several years hosted monthly overnight brainstorming sessions for leading business people at his cabin in the North Georgia mountains. He is a member of Vistage, the world's foremost chief executive leadership organization, frequently meeting to discuss strategy with local CEOs.

Steve Beecham

11855 Haynes Bridge Road,

Alpharetta GA 30009

steve@hometownmoney.com

www.bassackwardbusiness.com

Made in the USA
Lexington, KY
21 July 2012